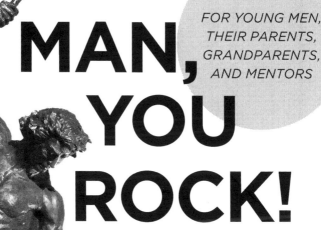

FOR YOUNG MEN, THEIR PARENTS, GRANDPARENTS, AND MENTORS

MAN, YOU ROCK!

12 Essential Life Skills to Build Your CHARACTER, VISION, AND FUTURE

Dr. REX S. VANDERWOOD

Foreword by *SELF MADE MAN* Sculptor **BOBBIE CARLYLE**

Man, You Rock!

For information about this title or to order other books and/or electronic media, contact the publisher:
Blackwatch Press, LLC
30 N. Gould St. Ste R, Sheridan, WY 82801
blackwatchpress.com
man-you-rock.com

Library of Congress Control Number: 2018906906
ISBN: 978-1-7323169-0-4 (Hardcover)
       978-1-7323169-1-1 (Softcover)
       978-1-7323169-2-8 (eBook)
       978-1-7323169-3-5 (Audio Retail Channels)
       978-1-7323169-4-2 (Audio Library Channels)

Printed in the United States of America
Cover and Interior design: 1106 Design, LLC

To:_____

From: _____

If you've received this book as a gift, it is the highest compliment because someone believes you have excellent potential, that you will inspire others, and that **"YOU, ROCK!"**

"The true measure of a man is not his physical appearance but rather the height of his vision, the depth of his character, and the width of his heart."

— REX S. VANDERWOOD

Contents

Principle #3   23
MANNERS AND ETIQUETTE

Principle #4   35
DRESS AND APPEARANCE

Principle #5   45
CHOOSE YOUR FRIENDS WISELY

Principle #6   51
EDUCATION

Foreword

OUR SUCCESS and prosperity as a nation and global community depend upon the success and prosperity of the family and each of us as individuals. This book is designed for the personal success and prosperity of each of us, by creating strong men of character — proper preparation is the key. This book is an easy-to-use handbook or step-by-step guide for sons (of all ages) and their parents, grandparents, and mentors. This book is also a must-have for single mothers raising sons.

So, when Dr. Rex Vanderwood asked me to write the foreword for *Man, You Rock! 12 Essential Life Skills to Build Your Character, Vision, and Future — For Young Men, Their Parents, Grandparents, and Mentors*, I was excited and honored, and immediately said, "Count me in!" Dr. Vanderwood explained to me his vision and inspiration in writing this book and how the *Self Made Man* sculpture had inspired his own life and desire for it to be the image for this book's cover. Our visions aligned perfectly, as the *Self Made Man* is a man carving himself out of stone, carving his character, carving his future. As a working professional and mother of seven children — as well as the creator/sculptor of the *Self Made Man* sculpture — I am thrilled to see this complete "instruction manual" for all of us to read and enjoy. Do so, and I promise you that it will literally change your life.

For more than three decades, Dr. Vanderwood has earned a stellar reputation in the service of his country, community, and his fellow man. His global influence, especially in humanitarian missions, has impacted literally thousands of men, women, and children around the world. He served 26 years in the United States Air Force, as a senior leader and commander. He has eight college degrees, including a doctorate in business administration. He is the managing partner of a successful strategic-consulting firm, highly sought-after speaker, but, of most importance, he is a husband, a son, a father, and a grandfather with a passion to help others to become their very best — the reason for this book.

This book is significant and timely, as surveys across the world consistently reveal that a parent's biggest hope is that their children will be happy, healthy, and successful. Yet, we live in a time in which families are under attack, being torn apart, divorce rates are at an all-time high, and children are all too often lacking the essential time, instruction, and development of life skills.

This book is a must-read in order to gain the critical life skills required to succeed — and the good news is that each of the 12 Principles/Life Skills can be learned.

No matter where you are in life, know this: The greater number of these 12 Principles/Life Skills you learn, the greater success in life you'll enjoy. Each principle is like a tool I use in creating my sculptures. Learn or pick up just one more tool (principle), and you will find greater success. Learn or pick up all these tools (12 principles), and you can create a masterpiece — you.

BOBBIE CARLYLE
Sculptor of the *Self Made Man*

Introduction

INSIDE THE pages of this book, an adventure awaits — an opportunity to become your very best self, the total package. Follow these 12 principles, and success will follow you.

UNIQUE — this is the only book ever written for young men and their parents, grandparents, and mentors focusing on "12 essential life skills" you must have to be successful in life. A special note to single mothers: Single mothers raising sons are an extraordinary force for good in shaping their life — this book will be an invaluable resource for you as well.

Life is often hard — especially for boys trying to make themselves into principled men. Those who lack a firm foundation of necessary "life skills" or who have few resources and mentors available to love and guide them have an even more difficult challenge when navigating life's choices. Today, even the best of young men are under constant attack and exposed to negative influences. Far too many boys are left on their own, disadvantaged, with a lack of focus and direction and trying to figure it out by chance. To become a great, respectable, and successful man seems "out of reach" to many.

Regardless of individual circumstances — where you live, your race, religion, age, height, weight, rich or poor, etc. — *Man, You Rock! 12 Essential Life Skills to Build Your Character, Vision, and Future — For Young Men, Their Parents, Grandparents, and Mentors* gives a step-by-step plan for **you** to become a success. As you read the following chapters, **you** will learn how to establish your **vision**, build your **character**, and refine your **manners** and **appearance**. Also, you will discover opportunity in **education**, the importance of having a **positive attitude**, and setting **priorities**. In addition, the value of **hard work**, **financial management**, and the importance of **health and fitness** are included. Furthermore, "must know" keys to **successful relationships** in **dating**, the absolute best proposal, and **best marriage** opportunity will all be yours — because, after reading these pages, you will have the knowledge to act upon these essential keys and be well on your way to **"Becoming That Kind of Man."**

EASY TO USE – each chapter gives short "how-to" answers to common questions, inspirational and humorous examples for each essential life skill, and a summarization of each principle. Concluding each chapter is a special section for "Parents, Grandparents, and Mentors," highlighting the point of that chapter with a small section depicting the current research on the topic. "Lessons/ Activities" provide invaluable "hands-on activities" specifically designed for parents, grandparents, or caring mentors to do with their sons and/or grandsons — to reinforce each essential life skill.

Becoming a great man is not about finding yourself but in "creating yourself." Starting with the first page, you can begin to change your life and provide yourself with a proven road map for becoming your very best self. Do not delay; isn't it time you joined the ranks of the most successful and happy men in the world? Simply turn the page and let the "new, best you" journey begin now. **It's a Fast Read. It's Simple to Understand. And It Works!**

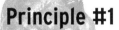

Principle #1

Vision: To Dream With Your Eyes Wide-Open

"All men dream, but not equally. Those who dream by night in the dusty recesses of their minds, wake in the day to find that it was vanity: but the dreamers of the day are dangerous men, for they may act on their dreams with open eyes, to make them possible."

— T. E. Lawrence

BEWARE OF DISTRACTIONS.
TAKE TIME TO THINK

THE TRUTH is that we live in a world of many distractions, lots of "fog" that clouds our vision and oftentimes our judgment. If we're not careful, we can end up in the wrong place, at the wrong time, doing the wrong thing. Therefore, sometimes, we need to "unplug" from our computer, video

1

games, cell phone, TV, music, etc., and "without distractions," just take time to think.

This is important, because it's your life, and it's your future. So take time to focus and think about "where" you want to be (right place), "when" you want to get there (right time), and "what" it is you really want (right thing). You need to create a clear vision of the "best you." In other words — dream with your eyes wide-open. Then it's time for action — it's time to become the successful man you want to be and can become.

> *"All of humanity's problems stem from man's inability to sit quietly in a room alone."*
>
> — Pascal

BEGIN WITH THE END IN MIND

Okay, so how many times have you heard your buddies say, "Yeah, when I grow up, I'm going to go to Harvard," or, "I'm going to be a doctor," or how about, "I'm going to be a professional basketball star in the NBA." *Question:* Although each is very admirable, what do these three things have in common? *Answer:* They're easy to say, yet extremely hard to do. Notice I did not say "impossible," as there are some people who actually go to Harvard University, become doctors, and are star NBA basketball players. So the next question is, "How did they do it?"

Here's some advice from Albert Einstein: "If I had an hour to solve a problem and my life depended on the solution, I would spend the first 55 minutes determining the proper question to ask, for once I know the proper question, I could solve the problem in less than five minutes." Wow! That's a lot of upfront preparation to get the answer to one's question, but then again, he said, "my life depended on the solution," and so it is with you: Your life depends on the solution — so you'd better take the time *now* to get it right. If you don't, you might hear your cousin Vinny say something like, "Well, he's a good guy, but he ain't no Einstein."

In real life, everybody is busy, running here, going there, doing this, and doing that, but doing something fast does not necessarily mean efficient, better, or even moving in the right direction. Yet, when someone is successful, others will naturally ask the question, "How did they do it?" Many people call it "luck," but luck has nothing to do with it. Rather, it is someone who had a dream, a vision — not of what they are today but what they could become. Meaning, they began the first steps of their journey "with the end in mind," and you can, too.

"There is no passion to be found in playing small — in settling for a life that is less than the one you are capable of living."

— Nelson Mandela

GOALS – CLEAR OR FUZZY?

I know what you're thinking: You've heard that having clearly defined goals in life will actually help you achieve them — right? But what's a "fuzzy goal"? Perhaps this example will help. Say two young men went off to the same college, best friends even, who grew up together in the same town, and one day they were talking about their dreams and goals in life. Let's say the first young man, named "Lax," said to his friend "Axe," "I want to buy my own house someday."

Axe then replied to his friend Lax, "I, too, desire to buy my own home and because I want to live in Seattle, I have looked at the price of starter homes in this area, I have researched the amount needed for a down payment, the trending interest rates, and the type of job I will need in order to save an amount of money between now and when I turn 25 to be able to buy my own home in Seattle."

Question: Which young man is most likely to achieve his goal of buying his own home? Lax's statement — "someday" — is a fuzzy goal. You see, just saying "someday" is the problem. Whereas Axe is as sharp as an axe and has a clear goal. They are defined and specific. He knows if he's going to have a home in Seattle that it is important to actually know what it will take to get it and when. This requires a step-by-step plan of action.

Oh, in case you're wondering just how things turned out? Several years later, Lax got jealous when Axe got the house, and now Axe refers to his former friend as "Ex-Lax"!

STEP-BY-STEP PLAN OF ACTION

You've heard the phrase "Talk is cheap." Well, it is not only cheap but also can be very annoying. The most successful people in the world "get this" and have not only a vision, clearly defined goals, and dreams, but they also have a plan of action, not just "big talk," but a step-by-step path to get there. Take the person who hopes to become a medical doctor. As much as they hope, hope, by itself, is not a good strategy. Hope is not going to get them there. But, the person who starts with the end in mind and identifies the education, dedication, and commitment of time and money required can then set up a step-by-step plan of action to get there. If they follow this proven strategy of success and take the necessary steps to get there, chances are they will be a doctor; if they don't, chances are they will not.

PICTURE (VISUALIZE) YOURSELF SUCCEEDING

It's important to develop a picture in your mind of you succeeding at whatever you're trying to accomplish. As an example, when I was 13, my dad bought a ski boat for our family to learn how to water ski. Although none of our family had ever tried waterskiing before, I was very excited to try. I remember, the night before our trip, I stayed awake and pictured (in my mind's eye) how it would be. I would be down in the water, my life jacket would keep me afloat while the tips of my skis were just sticking out of the water. Holding firmly onto the rope, I would then yell "Hit it, Dad!" At this point, I would let the boat pull me up on top of the water, and then I'd be skiing. I kept picturing these steps and how great it would be, how the crowds of people watching me on the beach would cheer, while some would even wonder, "What's a professional water-skier doing here?" I played this scenario over and over again in my mind, and, sometime during the night, I fell asleep.

The next morning, we hit the lake and launched the boat. This was going to be the greatest day of my life. My dad wanted to show the family "how waterskiing was to be done" so he jumped in, got all ready, and shouted, "Hit it!" But, to my great surprise, he didn't get up. He tried several times and could not pull himself up. My older brother jumped in … and experienced the same disappointing results. By this time, I was near having my first panic attack: If my strong father and likewise tough brother couldn't do it, why could I? But I remembered my picture of me doing it; I thought of each step, and I thought, *Well, I am at least going to try.* I jumped in, kept thinking about how I would do this, and, to my utter astonishment, *I DID IT!*

Although I was just 13, I learned a very valuable lesson that day; that it's not always about one's physical strength but one's mental strength or preparation. You've got to literally picture yourself succeeding at that which you desire to do and/or become. It doesn't really matter if it's waterskiing, academics at school, your job, or your relationships. I have found that, picturing yourself succeeding, in advance of trying, and, likewise, not giving up just because others have failed, has been a huge lesson and benefit throughout my entire life.

All Great Men Begin With A Vision, Not What They Are Today, But Rather Who They Will Become

For Parents, Grandparents, and Mentors

- **The Point:**
  Actively become this person yourself by taking time to think. Begin with the end in mind, and set clear goals aligned with your step-by-step plan of action. Then picture yourself succeeding. Likewise, help others along the way, especially your family and friends.

- **Studies Show:**
  "Studies consistently show that this one factor, personal vision, is more important in both success and satisfaction than any other factor — more important than intelligence, socioeconomic background, or education." (Highlands Company, 2017).

- **Lesson/Activity:**
  The Ordinary or the Prize Rose? Here's an easy but profound experiment and lesson for parents and grandparents to share with their respective sons and/or grandsons. I recommend doing each step together. First, preferably in the early Spring, go purchase two rose bushes, such as the hybrid tea rose, at your local nursery or garden center. Plant them in your yard, and follow the basic care and watering instructions

exactly the same for both plants. As both plants begin to grow and develop leaves and small buds, have your son and/or grandson select their future prize-winning rose by first selecting which bush and then second, select which of the many small buds on that bush will become the prize rose. Third, remove all of the other small rosebuds by pinching them off carefully with your fingers, leaving just one rosebud on this plant. Allow the other rose bush to keep all of its many rosebuds.

What happens over the next couple of weeks is almost magical. The rose bush with many roses will provide many "average-sized" roses. Whereas, the other rose bush, with only one rose, will bloom and grow much larger and more beautiful to become the "prize rose." Ask your son and/or grandson "why" this happened. Depending on their age and ability to make the connection, they may get it, or you may need to help explain this simple truth:

a) Out of all the many options, they chose the prize rose.

b) Luck had nothing to do with it. Any rose they chose would have grown into the prize rose, because,

c) By deliberately removing all of the other rosebuds, the one selected rosebud received all of the nutrients and minerals, whereas, the other rose bush shared the nutrients and minerals with all of the other roses.

d) The lesson. Just as in life, when you have the right vision to concentrate and prioritize your energies into something of your choice, you can grow and become great, like the prize rose. If you do not have the vision to concentrate and prioritize, you most likely will be average, like the average rose who gets little attention with no extra resources to help it become great.

Principle #2

Carve/Create Your Character

*"You cannot dream yourself into a character,
you must hammer and forge yourself one."*

— Henry David Thoreau

WHAT MANNER OF MAN OUGHT YOU TO BE?

THE TRUE measure of a man is not his physical appearance but rather the height of his vision, the depth of his character, and the width of his heart.

GOOD, BETTER, BEST – STRIVE FOR EXCELLENCE

Let's discuss the word "quality" for just a minute. Some things are just bad (no, not the slang hip "cool bad" or "sick" kind of "cool bad," but the less-than-good bad), whereas some things are good,

11

some better, and still others are best. We hear it all the time, and we make choices about quality constantly, some big, some small, but we each make daily decisions throughout our entire life.

As an example, think about all the automobile ads on TV. In just 30 seconds, we're told about how their cars are "more reliable, dependable, strong and durable, yet efficient with a loyal following" and that they're "#1 in quality and customer satisfaction 7 years in a row!" Wow, notice that all the "best" possible "characteristics" are mentioned in describing their certain car. Makes you notice — a standout performer from the crowded field of other cars. Makes you want to buy one — right? Now, can you imagine the very next commercial is a different automobile company advertising their car in this manner? "Hey, it works, okay, sometimes, not really efficient or dependable, but some people buy one. Why not you?"

Whaaaaaat? How ridiculous would it be for anyone to ever buy a car from this company with such lousy characteristics and poor quality? Yet, people are much like this car illustration. As their spelling and meaning imply, there is a close link between the words "characteristic" and "character," which is to say a noticeable quality of someone or something serving to identify it. How do we want to be identified? Shouldn't the greatest question we ask ourselves concerning our personal character be, "What manner of man should I be?" Or, said another way, "Do I want my life to be bad, or to be good, better, or why not best?" Strive for excellence, as this is who you are. It's your character, and it's how others will view you. The choice is yours, and you'll be making it every day.

BUILDING A STRONG FOUNDATION

Your character is "your" foundation. It's what you're built upon. For example, take a look at the cover of this book. The world-famous sculptor Bobbie Carlyle depicts the *Self Made Man* carving his "character" out of "stone." This is not by chance, by luck, or by accident, but rather a very deliberate choice to use stone. So the next question is "Why?" Meaning, wouldn't it be much easier to carve one's character out of a softer material, such as wood, clay, or even mud? Easier, yes; better or best, not even close.

Just as the *Self Made Man* sculpture was carved from stone, one chisel from the hammer at a time, we, too, must deliberately choose what we're made of and the price we're willing to pay in order to become this exceptional man. Whose character, if built upon a strong foundation, will weather the storms of life.

YOUR THOUGHTS, WORDS, ACTIONS, HABITS, CHARACTER – YOUR DESTINY

How many decisions does an adult person make on an average day? Studies show about 35,000 every day, and further studies at Cornell University reveal that we make around 226 decisions each day on food choices alone! That's a lot of choices and further solidifies that, truly, what we put in is what we get out. Our very thoughts, words, and actions *do* become our habits, while our habits become our character — it's then who we *are*.

Stephen Covey said it this way: "Our character is basically a composite of our habits. Because they are consistent, often unconscious patterns, they constantly, daily, express our character."

> *"Watch your thoughts; they become words.*
> *Watch your words; they become actions.*
> *Watch your actions; they become habits.*
> *Watch your habits; they become character.*
> *Watch your character; it becomes your destiny."*
>
> — Margaret Thatcher

RESPECTING YOUR PARENTS, FAMILY, FRIENDS, EVERYONE – AND YOURSELF

Billy Graham once said, "A child who is disrespectful to his parents will not have true respect for anyone." My father taught me this lesson and used a teaching moment very early in life when he said to me, "Son, the friend you just had over to play referred to his mother as his '… old lady ….' Let me be very clear: you will never refer to your mother as your 'old lady,' and, for that matter, you will never even think about calling me your 'old man'! Why? Because your mother deserves your greatest respect. She makes countless sacrifices every single day to help you grow up to become a person who is respectable, someone others will want to be around — someone to be proud of."

Throughout the years, I have often reflected upon the words of my father, and he was absolutely right. Those who showed respect for their parents, family, friends, and everyone around them, even when they disagreed, had a great advantage over those who did not. In life, there will be many people with whom you disagree. The difference in one's character is how you go about it, or the choice and actions of being either respectful or disrespectful. Through all of this, you must also respect yourself — be true to who you are.

YOUR WORD IS YOUR BOND, YOUR REPUTATION – IT'S WHO YOU ARE

Whether you know it or not, you are building a reputation through your words and your actions. In order to illustrate this point, let's say, for example, your parents ask you to take out the trash, load and unload the dishwasher, and mow the lawn today; you say, "Sure. No problem." Although there are other things you wanted to do, you decided to do what your parents asked you to do first. This is not only doing the right thing by being responsible, obedient, dependable, and trustworthy, but you're also building "your reputation" as someone others can count on. In other words, your word is your bond.

Meaning, when you commit or promise to do something or for someone, you do it. In contrast, someone who does not keep their word breaks promises and is not someone you can count on. The same is true with someone who is dishonest, lies, cheats, or bullies others. They, too, are building their reputation but, unfortunately, in a negative way. It takes inner strength and courage to rise above, to be honest and kind — as kindness is the signature of a true gentleman — a rock-solid man of character.

So, how does your reputation affect your character? Reputation is what you do when someone is watching. Character is what you do when no one is watching. Character, your character, is what determines how you will react to and confront the most difficult and challenging trials and opportunities in life. Remember, building your reputation and character is a choice, and the choice is yours.

> *Your Character Will Determine How You Will Weather The Storms Of Life*

For Parents, Grandparents, and Mentors

◆ **The Point:**
This principle on *character* is perhaps the most important of all principles in this book. It establishes the very core of who we are and what we represent. Therefore, it is of vital importance to be the "best" example, role model, mentor, etc. There is no substitute for being a man of character, as your strength of character or lack thereof will speak much more loudly than words. What is the universal biggest hope and dream as parents? To raise our children to have an even better life than our own; to accomplish this requires time — not what's left over after everything else but the best you have to offer.

◆ **Studies Show:**
"A review of more than 10,000 sons and daughters in 36 separate studies around the world concluded that a cold or distant father can damage a child's life, sometimes for decades to come ... Professor Rohner, of the University of Connecticut, added that research shows the same parts of the brain are activated when people feel rejected as when they suffer physical pain. He added, however, that unlike

physical pain, people can psychologically relive the emotional pain of rejection over and over for years." (Macrae, 2012)

The research shows that the input of a strong father figure is particularly important in developing and influencing their sons, because it is quite natural for a young boy to look up to this father figure and say, "When I grow up, I want to be just like you." When your influence is positive, it generally produces positive results. However, if your influence is negative, passive, and/or nonexistent, the statistics are alarming.

◆ **Statistics:**
- 63% of youth suicides are from fatherless homes — 5 times the average (US Department of Health/Census)
- 90% of all homeless and runaway children are from fatherless homes — 32 times the average
- 85% of all children who show behavior disorders come from fatherless homes — 20 times the average (Centers for Disease Control)
- 80% of rapists with anger problems come from fatherless homes — 14 times the

average (*Justice & Behavior*, Vol 14, p. 403–26)

* 71% of all high school dropouts come from fatherless homes — 9 times the average (National Principals Association Report)

◆ Lesson/Activity:

Choices—Which Path to Take. Parents, take your son(s), and/or grandparents, take your grandson(s) on a hike. Together, be certain to select a venue — whether it is hiking in the mountains, a state or national park, or your nearby city park — that is appropriate for their and your physical-ability level. Keep safety at the forefront as you plan and do the following:

a) Pre-hike Plan — take time together to select a date and time and a place to hike. If you can get a map of your hiking routes, pick up or download the map.

b) Next, take time together to plan your hike. Highlight the paths you will take by marking this route on your map.

c) Then, list the supplies you will need in order to successfully complete your hike, such as map, water, food (snacks and/or meals), backpack to carry supplies, compass, proper clothing, shoes or boots, first-aid kit, etc.

Enjoy your hike; enjoy your time together. This activity provides you with not only some exercise (physical activity) and, most importantly, quality time together but also some fantastic teaching-moment opportunities along the way. Whether it's the summit on the mountaintop, sitting by a cool river, or just a quiet, peaceful setting by the trees, consider these points as a lesson on character:

a) As in life, this hike (our journey today) provides many different paths to take ... some good, some better, and others best.

b) Before we started our journey today, we selected the best route. It was our decision — not someone else's but ours. We looked at all the many paths and chose the best one.

c) We also made preparations for our journey in having supplies (food, water, map, etc.) to take with us and help us along the way.

d) We made it to the top of the mountain, the summit, our desired destination, not by chance or by luck, but rather by our deliberate choice. We started out with a map (plan) of how to get there, the important supplies needed along the way, and we *made it!*

e) In your own words, express the similarities of this adventure to life — from planning, to doing, to succeeding is like building your son's or grandson's character and future. He, too, will need a map (plan) to be the best; then, at each step along life's path, he will choose the right one, follow the map, stay on the path, and become the "best" man he can become.

f) Parents and grandparents, the most important thing you can do is to express your love and support for your son and/or grandson. They need to know how proud you are of them, even when they make a bad decision and go down the wrong path. They have to know that you will be there for them and help them along life's journey. In short, they must be accountable and responsible for their own decisions and actions, but they can always count on your unconditional love as a foundational cornerstone throughout their entire life.

Principle #3
Manners and Etiquette

"Good manners have much to do with the emotions. To make them ring true, one must feel them, not merely exhibit them."

— Amy Vanderbilt

A TIME TO SPEAK, A TIME TO LISTEN – KNOW THE DIFFERENCE

I REMEMBER a certain "large and in charge" fourth-grader from when I was just 10 years old. One day, while on recess outside on the playground, just hanging with my other fourth-grade peeps, a very nice girl and her friends from our class approached me and said, "Hi, Rex. I heard that your mother is pregnant." Well, being completely unaware of what the word "pregnant" meant, I just knew that it didn't sound good, hardly a compliment. So in defending my dear mother, yet in my ignorance, I immediately replied (in a rather loud fourth-grader voice), *"Oh, no, she isn't — you are!"* Needless to say, she (and all of my now most-likely never future dates) just shook their heads and walked away. Gentlemen, when you don't know what you're talking about — keep your mouth shut! Mark Twain once said, "Better to remain silent and be thought a fool than to speak and to remove all doubt." That particular day, I absolutely removed all doubt. Nevertheless, sometimes in our life, it is best to apologize to the person we've offended by learning when to say "I'm sorry."

SAYING, "I'M SORRY"

A gentleman knows when and how to sincerely apologize. For example, when you say something stupid and hurt someone's feelings, or when you show up late for a date or a dinner invitation, or perhaps you broke or lost something that a friend lent you. It's time to apologize. Although everyone makes mistakes, it is a responsible gentleman who knows how to make it right. It's important to realize that, in some circumstances, it's not enough to just say you're sorry — you need to take further steps to replace that which you have broken or lost. The key is to learn from your mistakes and do your best not to make them again. The consequences of "habitual stupidity" (making stupid a habit) are a rapid loss of friends, dates, and/or dinner invitations — not good!

Oh, and to Denise, although it's been 40+ years since I told you (in the fourth grade) that *you* were pregnant and not my mother — I am sorry. I was wrong. She was very much pregnant at the time, and I have a lovely sister as a result. Please accept my apology for this misunderstanding.

Note to Fathers: Please read Parents, Grandparents, and Mentors section on the appropriate time to discuss "the Birds and the Bees" with your son. He'll thank you for it later, and, quite possibly, you'll save him great embarrassment.

SAYING "PLEASE" AND "THANK YOU"

Saying "Please" and "Thank you" go together like cookies and milk, peanut butter and jelly, or macaroni and cheese! It's just the right thing to do. Here's why: Say you're being interviewed for a really great job. The employer says to you that, although they have just one position or job opening available, it's between you and one other person for the job. She tells you that both of you have the same qualifications and that she'll make the final decision depending on this interview.

You and the other guy go to the interview. You're both dressed appropriately and look prepared to seal the deal and get the job. You're called into her office first, and she greets you with a nice welcome and asks if you'd like to take a seat. You reply, "Yes, please, and thank you — it is very nice to meet you as well." 10 minutes later, when the other guy is greeted and is asked the same question, he says, "Yeah." At the end of the interview, she thanks you for your time and suggests that she'll make a decision and let you know by tomorrow afternoon. You reply, "I'd like to thank you for this tremendous opportunity and look forward to hearing from you and being a part of this team." The other guy's response is just, "Okay." Now, with all other things being equal, who do you think got the job? Who was by far more impressive, well-mannered, prepared, confident, successful, etc.? You are — because a gentleman knows that his manners are a reflection of who he is and how he treats others, everyone — with kindness, dignity, and respect.

THE GOLDEN RULE

Do unto others as you would have them do unto you — that is to say, have a genuine concern for others, and treat all people with kindness, dignity, and respect. Martin Luther King, Jr. said, "You can easily judge the character of a man by how he treats those who can do nothing for him."

SHAKING HANDS

You may have sometimes fantasized about being like NBA great LeBron James and going down the line to give your fellow teammates a series of elaborate pregame mega-shakes. It's very entertaining and looks somewhat like a well-rehearsed mini-ballet, with their hands waving and slapping, fingers wiggling high, then low, then the finale shake, which ends like a fireworks display as he spins, twirls, and moves off to the next player. It's really cool if you're "King James" putting on a performance at the basketball arena, but if you're not him, please pay particular attention here.

The entire rest of mankind should keep it simple. A gentleman's handshake should be firm and strong, but not crushing. A couple pumps and no more. It's also a good idea to look at the person in the eyes and extend a confident greeting, such as, "Hello. My name is (your name). It's a pleasure to meet you." Or, if you're seeing someone you already know, you might say, "Hi (their name). It's great to see you again. How's your golf game these days?" And one more thing: remember that a gentleman always waits for a lady to extend her hand before he offers to shake her hand.

There's good news and bad news. The good news — follow these simple handshake rules, and others will most certainly be impressed. The bad news — ignore the simple handshake and start your hands waving, fingers wiggling high and low, and others, especially older adults, might dial 911! Please, just keep it simple, as almost everyone will appreciate it.

OPENING THE DOOR FOR OTHERS

A gentleman opens doors for ladies, regardless of their age, young and old alike, it's the right thing to do. Why is this? It may seem old-fashioned, and some may even tell you that they can open their own door. If this is the case, it's probably best to let them. However, do not then assume that you're "off the hook" with this important manner. It is much more likely that this gesture will be greatly appreciated and that you will receive genuine compliments about being such a fine gentleman.

Okay — so, then, what about men? Do you open the door for them, too? The short answer is "Yes." For example, you would not open the front door at your home for your mother and sister but let it shut in front of your brother and/or the face of your father. A gentleman remembers the "Golden Rule" and treats *everyone* with kindness, dignity, and respect.

TELEPHONE ETIQUETTE

A gentleman never answers the phone with, "What up?" "Wussup? "Sup?" or even "Yello, yo!" Unless your friend's nickname is "Pigpen" or "Cockroach," it's just not right. What is right is answering in a clear speaking voice — meaning nothing is in your mouth — and saying, "Hello. This is (your name)." If the call is not for you, and you're at work and they ask for your boss, an appropriate response would be, "Yes, certainly. May I ask who's calling?" Then you'll look good to your boss when you walk up to him and say, "Mr. Vanderbilt, there's a call for you from Mr. Rockefeller on line one." This is much more impressive than saying, "Uh, yeah, big guy — there's somebody on the phone who wants you."

INTERNET, E-MAILS, CELL PHONES, AND SOCIAL MEDIA

A gentleman knows that technology can be a wonderful thing if used properly, but likewise, he knows it can be a living nightmare if abused.

Rule #1 is when you put anything on the internet, e-mails, text messages, social media posts, etc, it's not private, and it lasts forever and ever. Rule #2 is always take time to think clearly about what you say in your posts, tweets, e-mails, and pictures you take, receive, and share — and then never forget Rule #1!

A GENTLEMAN AT THE DINNER TABLE

If you've been invited to someone's home for dinner, it's important that you confirm your attendance at your earliest convenience, as they will need time to plan for the food, seating arrangements, etc. A gentleman takes a small gift to show his appreciation to the host and hostess. It can be as simple as flowers, a box of chocolates, or a dessert. He's punctual, that is to say, he arrives on time; he also dresses appropriately for the occasion. At a more formal dinner, jeans and a T-shirt will make a statement, but not the one you'll want others to remember about you. If you're uncertain about the dress, inquire ahead of time. This will potentially save you lots of embarrassment.

Prior to being seated, ensure that your hands are washed. Wait for the host or hostess to tell you where to sit. Before taking your seat, stand in back of your chair until all the ladies in the room have been seated. You may even pull their chair out and assist them if a lady is seated next to you. Place your napkin in your lap, but do not begin eating until the host and hostess begin. Keep your elbows off the table. Don't reach, but wait for the food to be passed to you. Utensils: start at the outside forks and spoons, and work in toward your plate. If uncertain, observe your host.

It's also important to chew your food with your mouth closed. Nothing will ruin another's appetite faster than watching — and most likely hearing — your food move around in your mouth while eating, or worse, talking with food in your mouth. Next, remember that polite conversation is also important. Talk about something of interest to the dinner guests invited. When finished eating, place your utensils in the center of your plate, not on the tablecloth. Wait for your host and hostess to stand and depart the dining room before you do. Compliments to the host and hostess for a wonderful dinner and evening are always appreciated.

WRITING A "THANK YOU" NOTE

As a gentleman, young and old, you should have your own "Thank You" cards. Having stationery with your own name on it is even more impressive. Why? Because throughout your entire life, you will receive gifts from others, have dinner invitations, and many other nice things others will do for you. Many times, just saying "Thank you" is enough, whereas other, more special occasions require a handwritten thank-you note. This behavior on your part shows that you have manners. It shows a maturity in you, that you recognize the time, effort, and/or expense someone has spent on you.

Unfortunately, these days, most men — and virtually no young men — even *think* about writing a thank-you note. While some men may not know any better, others may know but just don't take the time and effort to actually do it. Manners, as are all matters of life, are a choice — you decide to either be selfish or selfless. A gentleman knows more than *how* to act properly with manners — he actually *does* it, and it becomes part of his character, as a way of life, each and every day.

Manners Are Like A Mirror: A Reflection Of Who You Are And What Others See

For Parents, Grandparents, and Mentors

◆ **The Point:**

Fred Astaire once said, "The hardest job kids face today is learning good manners without seeing any." This is where your example is of vital importance. Your children and grandchildren will be far more likely to exhibit good manners if they are in an environment that constantly displays and reinforces good manners.

One final point to all the father figures: the "Birds and the Bees" talk is one of your biggest and most important responsibilities. Do not "opt out" of this discussion, ask your spouse to do it, or even worse, assume that your son will figure it out. The truth is that he will have many people willing to influence his life; the most important influence regarding his morality, health, safety, and future should come from his father figure. If you are a single parent, you may have to assume this responsibility.

◆ **Studies Show:**

A recent study by cultureandyouth.org found that teens have quite a few things to say about appropriate manners and etiquette:

* 91% of teens say that manners and etiquette are important in their lives.

* 70% of teens feel society as a whole displays more bad manners than good.

* 97% of teens say they learn their manners from home.

◆ **Lesson/Activity:**
Young Men's Night Out. After your son or grandson has read this part of the book on "manners and etiquette," take him out for a nice dinner. This will not only give you some great quality time together, but you'll also provide him with the opportunity to "practice" his manners. The key here is to be patient. Go have some fun together, but also take this opportunity to teach and mentor. If you need to, take this book with you and discuss over dinner some of the other sections on being a gentleman such as shaking hands, saying "Please" and "Thank you," as well as writing thank-you notes. Note: this would be an excellent time to present him with his own note cards and/or stationery with his name printed on them. It's like going from boy to man—a rite of passage in growing up and being well-mannered.

Principle #4

Dress and Appearance

"The first step to being respected is to look respectable."

— Being Caballero

LOOK SHARP, ACT SHARP, BE SHARP

THE U.S. Armed Services have their respective Basic Military Training Centers, better known as "boot camps." Every week, this is where new recruits come pouring in from every state and territory, from every walk of life with diverse values, cultures, and attitudes. Upon arrival, these young men and women not only act different, they look different; from their clothes to the length of their haircuts. On day one, everyone is issued their military uniforms. Men receive the exact same haircut, which is to say, "All hair, long or short, hits the floor." What happens over the next few weeks is truly remarkable and inspiring.

Picture a graduation ceremony, unlike any other, on a military parade ground. Hundreds of young men and women are dressed in their full military dress uniforms, all of them moving as one. They march precisely to the beat of the ceremonial drums and band playing with perfect precision, as the many families and friends admire in awe in the grandstands. The transformation is remarkable. These great Americans, regardless of their backgrounds, race, religion, culture, rich or poor not only provide the backbone of America's defense but also prove this basic fact: When you *look* sharp, you *act* sharp, and then you'll *be* sharp. I know this to be true because I was one of them.

DRESS FOR SUCCESS

Gentlemen, you never get a second chance to make a first impression. First impressions matter, so make yours a great one. How's this done? By dressing appropriately for the occasion — meaning, wearing the proper clothes at the right time and in the right place. This does not imply that you must wear the most expensive clothes or that you should always be in a coat and tie. No, you may want to be in old jeans and a T-shirt while mowing the lawn, or watching the football game on Saturday afternoon. However, this attire may not be your best "first impression" and most likely would be your "last impression" on, say, a nice date or job interview. Nevertheless, it is important to note, you can dress a pig in a tuxedo, and you know what he is? That's right — he's still a pig. Your dress and appearance matter; it's a point of refinement. But, never forget: being a true gentleman requires a solid character beneath the clothes. The ultimate goal here is to transform into the total package — the "best" you can be — and this includes knowing how to properly and appropriately dress for the occasion.

THE INFORMAL TO THE FORMAL – CASUAL, SMART CASUAL, SUIT AND TIE, TO BLACK TIE

So many options, but not to worry. Here's a quick recommendation guide of what's best to wear for the occasion. First, if you've received an invitation to a luncheon, dinner, party, wedding reception, or other similar events, the invitation will usually list the recommended dress. Here are some examples:

– *Casual* — Wear shorts, jeans, or cargo pants and a T-shirt if you wish. Just remember, "casual" means "casual" — not dirty, soiled, or even wrinkled. Be clean — you and your clothes. Also, absolutely no one wants to see your undies—shorts and pants. "Pull 'em up," as you do not want to be the "butt" of family, friends, and neighbors' jokes!

- *Smart Casual* — Leave your jeans, tennis shoes, and baseball cap at home. Instead, wear khakis or chino pants, a collared shirt such as a golf/polo or dress shirt with nicer shoes and belt. Add a sports jacket or blazer if you want to be more formal.

- *Suit and Tie* — A gentleman, regardless of age, has a suit and tie. You'll want to dress appropriately for not only church, funerals, and weddings, but also for other formal occasions, including a job interview, a nice date, or even your normal workday. There are lots of different suit-and-tie options. Learn how to tie your own tie and shine your own dress shoes, and ensure that your suit, tie, pocket square (optional), belt, shirt, shoes, and socks look good together. For example, white gym socks with any suit combo are just not right!

- *Black Tie* — This means a fancy event, usually beginning after 6:00 pm, to which men wear a tuxedo. Common examples are formal dances, formal weddings, and/ or formal entertaining. A gentleman may rent or buy his own "tux," depending upon his frequency of going "black tie" formal.

HANDKERCHIEFS VERSUS USING YOUR SLEEVE

A gentleman carries a clean handkerchief. Here are several really good reasons why. We all sneeze. Without being too graphic, this natural occurrence can and does sometimes get really messy. A handkerchief can help. You need to clean your cell phone or your glasses. A handkerchief can help. Now, men, pay close attention here. You're at church, a funeral, or you're watching *The Titanic*, *A Walk to Remember*, or *Old Yeller* with your date. They begin to cry (more on you crying later); you pull out a clean, dry handkerchief with your initials on it and gently hand it to them. You have not only helped, but your chivalrous act as a gentleman will surely be remembered and will set you apart from the countless boys who have nothing to offer but their sleeve. See the difference?

PERSONAL HYGIENE, FINGERNAILS, HAIRCUT, COLOGNE/AFTERSHAVE

According to practically every study ever done since the Stone Age, the #1 biggest turn-off is a man's "long, dirty, or unkempt fingernails." In other words, if others mistake you for a Hobbit from *Lord of the Rings*, you need to dust off your nail clippers and use them! Seriously, if you're old enough to read this book, you're old enough to keep up with your own personal hygiene. This means, on a very regular basis, you should bathe/shower, brush and floss your teeth, use mouthwash, keep finger and toenails trimmed, use deodorant/antiperspirant, and keep your hair cut and trimmed.

Now, while on the subject of hair, here's a simple rule — keep it clean. Shave, or if you have a beard, you should also keep it clean and trimmed. Sometimes, men have unwanted "extra hair" growing from our nostrils and ears. If you do, don't panic, you can remedy this issue with an inexpensive nose and ear-hair trimmer. Like your toothbrush, it works great, but only when you use it.

A huge note on men's cologne and aftershave: Gentlemen, use it sparingly. The ultra-large bottle of "Hai Karate" aftershave your Aunt Jody gave you for your birthday was never intended to be splashed on your body. When you use any cologne or aftershave, it is always best if applied in a single mist you can walk through, not a tidal wave. If you use a strongly scented deodorant or body spray, it should match your cologne. Always remember, your cologne is never a substitute for your good hygiene of being fresh and clean.

Manners And Fine Clothes Are A Sign Of Refinement, Yet Are Only Building Blocks In Becoming A True Gentleman

For Parents, Grandparents, and Mentors

- ### The Point:

  There's a common metaphorical phrase, "You can't judge a book by its cover." This is to say that one should not prejudge someone or something solely on the basis of outward appearance, as it may not be a reliable indication of its true character. This is sound wisdom, as one's character (inside) is far more important than one's features (outside). Yet, we live in a world which is very visually oriented. Likewise, we make initial judgments and form opinions on how something looks every day, and that includes the way we dress. In keeping with this metaphor, if the book cover represents a person's cover, or dress and appearance, it is worth noting that even the greatest books ever written will most likely not be read if they lack a good cover. Likewise, the best people in the world (character) will most likely not be received well if they lack a good cover (dress, hygiene, and appearance). It is the total package that leads to the greatest opportunities. Think good, better, and best. Your personal example, teaching, and mentoring will most likely lead your son and/or grandson to become their best — inside and out.

◆ **Studies Show:**

"Research shows that your appearance strongly influences other people's perception of your financial success, authority, trustworthiness, intelligence, and suitability for hire or promotion" (*Business Insider*, 2014).

◆ **Lesson/Activity:**

All Dressed Up — A Night on the Town. Parents and grandparents, here's a perfect opportunity for you to take your son and/or grandson out on the town. This lesson/activity is in three separate phases. First, preparation. Select an upcoming special performance or event, and secure the tickets. It's great if it's something the entire family would enjoy. Then, make a list together of the proper attire required for your special event. Let's say a nice new suit and tie are appropriate, and then go shopping together and buy the suit with accessories. If this includes leather shoes, include a shoe-polishing kit. If there are budget concerns, great suits can often be purchased at second-hand stores. Second, well in advance of the event, teach your son and/or grandson how to tie his own tie and how to polish and care for his dress shoes. It's important to do some "show and tell," be patient, and praise even the smallest success to encourage confidence. Depending upon his age, it may also be an ideal time to reiterate the importance of good hygiene, and manners as referenced in this book. Third, get all dressed up, and take your son and/or grandson (family) out on the town. Enjoy the event and entire evening together. Be sure to take pictures, as you will want to reinforce this behavior and encourage future positive events and memories.

Principle #5
Choose Your Friends Wisely

"Choose your friends with caution; plan your future with purpose and frame your life with faith."

— Thomas S. Monson

RISE UP – STAND ABOVE THE CROWD

CHRISTOPHER REEVE once said, "What makes Superman a hero is not that he has power, but that he has the wisdom and the maturity to use the power wisely." Some people don't believe in heroes, but they're there. Perhaps they don't wear a superhero uniform like Superman, Iron Man, or Spider-Man, but they're there. In real life, these are the few ordinary people who do extraordinary things. While others sit down, they rise up. While others work to get the best position in the crowd, they stand above the crowd. Likewise, as you choose your friends from a crowded field, have the wisdom and maturity to look up, not down. Be very cautious and select extraordinary friends, with the highest standards and character. As you do, you will begin to "rise up" above the crowd and become somebody else's hero.

PEER PRESSURE – DON'T DO IT JUST BECAUSE IT'S POPULAR OR A FAD

Often, you will feel "peer pressure," or in other words, pressure from others to do something that you're not comfortable with. It would be great if you could have a bright sign flash in front of you that says something like, "Caution — Peer Pressure" or "Caution — Your Future Is Ahead. Make the Right Choices." Fortunately, each of us has a conscience — the part of our mind that makes us aware of what is right and wrong in our thoughts and actions. So, essentially, we do have signs or warnings, but it takes courage to follow them and choose the right way. Remember that "Wrong is wrong, even if everyone is doing it. Right is right, even if no one is doing it."

WILLING TO WALK ALONE

What's better? To have tons of friends that you follow around and do whatever they do or you carefully select your friends and at times you may even be alone, but remain true to yourself? It is better for you to walk alone than to simply follow the crowd leading you in the wrong direction. This is a major sign of growing from boy to man. *You* decide "now" who you are, your vision for your life, your values and character — indeed, your future. Do not wait until someone tries leading you in the wrong direction to make your decision. Always remember who you are, and be willing, if necessary, to walk alone.

SURROUND YOURSELF WITH THE BEST PEOPLE – FRIENDS AND ROLE MODELS

Oprah Winfrey said, "Surround yourself only with people who will lift you higher." This is great advice because the best people will encourage, motivate, and elevate you higher; average people will probably let you down. Why is this so vitally important? Because the friends you choose will be the friends you spend time with. The friends you spend time with will have great influence on the choices you make, and the choices you make will determine your life.

> *If You Desire To Be Successful, Surround Yourself With Successful People*

For Parents, Grandparents, and Mentors

- **The Point:**

  Remember when we were kids? For some of us, it seems very long ago. Regardless, it is fair to say that we made some dumb mistakes and that perhaps many of these happened when we were with our friends. Now, we have our own children, and some of us are even blessed to have grandchildren. A *New York Times* article reveals, "The lesson is that if you have a kid whom you think of as very mature and able to exercise good judgment, based on your observations when he or she is alone or with you, that doesn't necessarily generalize to how he or she will behave in a group of friends without adults around. Parents should be aware of that." Meaning, even the *best* of kids can be influenced by their friends. Therefore, encouraging them to associate with the *best* of friends is of paramount importance.

- **Studies Show:**

  Your friends influence you; this observation is backed by science. *"You're likely to start acting like the people you surround yourself with. Pick friends who make poor choices, and you could get dragged down fast. But, if you choose friends who inspire and challenge you to become better, you'll increase your chances of reaching your goals."* (Morin, 2015)

◆ **Lesson/Activity:**
Developing Future Heroes. Parents and grand-parents, take time out of your busy schedule to spend some more quality time with your son(s) or grandson(s) individually, one-on-one. Don't underestimate the power and influence of a role model and mentor in their young lives. Start by selecting a private location without a lot of distractions, allowing them to truly focus. First, ask them who their heroes are, and then ask why. After this discussion, talk with them about their life, and perhaps highlight the positive traits and characteristics they have shown, such as being: smart, honest, helpful, considerate, and strong (physically, mentally, morally), for example. Next, relate their strengths to the heroes in their lives. In other words, help them see just how similar they are to their heroes and how proud you are that they're making choices to be such a great man. Finally, ask them about their friends and discuss whether their friends lift them up and inspire them, or do they make poor choices and bring them

down. Lovingly explain the direct relationship of their friends' possible influence over them and the importance of choosing their friends wisely as to grow up and become somebody else's real-life hero.

Principle #6
Education

"The function of education is to teach one to think intensively and to think critically. Intelligence plus character — that is the goal of true education."

— Martin Luther King, Jr.

DO WELL IN SCHOOL – EDUCATION
OPENS DOORS TO YOUR FUTURE

"ACCORDING TO your abilities, this math class will be divided into three separate groups. When I call your name, the top students will go into the gold room." Names were called, but not mine. The teacher then said, "Next, when I call your name, the majority of you will please go into the blue room." Again, names were called, but not mine. Now, there were only a few kids left sitting in our chairs, heads down, shoulders slumping, when he finally said; "Okay, the rest of you need to go into the red room." *The red room!* I was so embarrassed and disappointed because I was now a "red room" guy. Clearly, this was the most embarrassing and challenging time in my young school life.

Unfortunately, from the fifth grade until I entered college, I believed that I was bad at math. I somehow did well in all other subjects, but not math. Why? Because I was labeled as a "red room" math guy, and I believed it. Well, at least until I married my lovely wife. She built me up; she gave me confidence; she told me that I was intelligent and that I could do well in math, and I believed her.

Here's the rest of the story. Because I now believed I could do well and I likewise worked really hard, I have since then earned multiple college degrees and have even tested out of statistics via CLEP exam, providing college credit without having to take the course. Come to find out, I really enjoy math, and I did not let my being labeled as "bad" at something keep me from my dreams and goals in life. I have learned from personal experience these two important lessons: First, don't let the words and/or actions of others "hold you down" or define you. Second, education is the key that unlocks the doors of opportunity, and opportunity is what everyone needs to succeed.

GET YOUR HIGH SCHOOL DIPLOMA – MORE THAN JUST A PIECE OF PAPER

America, for example, is known around the world as a great land of opportunity, but for those who decide to drop out of high school, that opportunity just got a lot harder. According to Johnson (2011), here are some facts to consider in the "costs of dropping out":

- Unemployment rate (no job) is twice as high for people without a high school diploma.

- Over a lifetime, a person without a high school diploma will earn $200,000 less than a high school graduate and nearly $1 million less than people who graduate from college.

- It's not just about fewer jobs and less money. High school dropouts are much more likely to commit crimes, go to prison, live in poverty, abuse drugs and alcohol, become teenage parents, etc.

The bottom line: stay in school, do the best you can, and earn your high school diploma.

COLLEGE (MORE EDUCATION)

If education is the key that unlocks the doors of opportunity, then going to college or a technical training school is the vehicle to get you there. Why is this? "College graduates, on average, earned 56% more than high school grads in 2015, according to data compiled by the Economic Policy Institute." The financial advantage of having a college education largely determines other important issues, such as where you live, the likelihood of owning a home, quality-of-life issues, etc. Besides the more traditional college path, many may do better by gaining job skills in areas increasingly in demand involving technology.

SELECTING A FIELD OF STUDY

Follow your passion, but all college degrees do not mean they all pay the same when you graduate. For example, according to government data, some healthcare jobs, such as a typical X-ray technician, earn around $60,000 a year, and that's with just a two-year college degree (*USA Today*, 2017). But the occupations related to many four-year liberal arts degrees, as wonderful as the education is, may not have the same job demand and therefore substantially limit one's earnings. Therefore, selecting your field of study requires a lot of thought, deliberate research, and planning. Perhaps some educational pursuits might be better as your hobby or interest, but not necessarily as your career.

PLANNING YOUR OCCUPATION – IT'S WHERE AND HOW YOU'LL SPEND A LOT OF YOUR LIFE

So what's the difference between simply getting jobs and or planning for your occupation and career? A job is doing work for some pay, whereas an occupation is more of a broad professional category of jobs, like being a teacher, plumber, accountant, doctor, or lawyer. It's also important to enjoy your work, otherwise as some may suggest, "It's Thursday — or as I like to call it — Day 4 of the hostage situation." But, back to the point: Just getting jobs every few months is very different from getting the required education and training and working within an occupation or field you enjoy and making it a career. With the former, you'll make a living. With the latter, you'll have a life.

CONSTANT IMPROVEMENT

Success in any aspect of life appears to follow those who constantly improve. For example, if you want to improve physically, by building bigger muscles, you must first learn how to do it — and then do it. Continual education + training = development. Likewise, you must learn to develop your mind to expand your thinking in all aspects of your life — beyond high school, college, etc. Just as going to the gym and lifting weights only "one time" and never going back will do little but most likely make you really sore and sweaty. No, in order to "develop and grow," you need to continue to go on a regular basis, making it a habit. Constant improvement is a lifetime endeavor—your education, training, and development should never stop.

Education Is The Key That Unlocks
The Door To Opportunity

For Parents, Grandparents, and Mentors

◆ **The Point:**

Education is what opens our minds and allows us to learn and grow. Therefore, getting the best education is vital to our lives, establishes a firm foundation for our future, and greatly affects our posterity. John Locke said, *"The improvement for understanding is for two ends: first, our own increase of knowledge; secondly, to enable us to deliver that knowledge to others."*

◆ **Studies Show:**

Recent studies show that although school is important, students spend just 15% of their time in school and that the parents' role and influence is much more important. For example, *"Parental involvement — checking homework, attending school meetings and events, discussing school activities at home — has a more powerful influence on students' academic performance than anything about the school the students attend."* Decades of research concludes this simple fact: if you want to give your children an edge — talk. Here's why. *"Professional parents talk more to their children than less-affluent parents — a lot more, resulting in a 30 million-word gap by the time children reach age three." TIME (2012)*

◆ **Lesson/Activity:**

Education—Essential for Life. Parents and grandparents, here's a simple but profound lesson you can teach your son(s) or grandson(s). This lesson/activity is a two-pronged approach; the first part is for a young boy or a teenager still living "at home." The second part focuses on his life after he moves "out of your home."

First, the "at home" phase. Start by asking him, "What's your favorite ice cream, movie, sports team, etc.?" After he responds, make the point that "he had the ability to choose what he wanted or preferred." Next, make the point that while he's growing up, he likewise has the ability to choose what type of job or profession he would prefer. Yet, unlike saying, "I choose chocolate ice cream," choosing your best job or profession requires a good education and that means doing well in school.

Share with him the importance of doing well in school. If he's doing well, be sure to recognize that, however, if he's not, discuss some ways that he can do better. Note, this may very well involve your help. Don't let him believe that he's just not smart enough, because most likely that's not the problem. During your school discussion, explain that there is another very important lesson that every young man should know, and that's learning "essential life skills."

Depending upon his age, this may include things like: making his bed, taking out the trash, setting the table, cooking (more than a microwave burrito), washing dishes, mowing the lawn, grocery shopping, budgeting money, ironing his own shirts, etc. Your role as parent and grandparent is to ensure that your son and/or grandson is prepared for how the "real world" works, before they're out in the middle of it. Learning the essential life skills is absolutely vital in preparing him in advance for developing his *mental toughness* to handle life when he's on his own.

Second, now discuss the "after he moves 'out of your home' phase." It's never too early to discuss his future, and that includes his career. For example, even if your son is only 12, it may very well be an appropriate time to help him see how his schooling and choices, in general, affect his life. Start out by asking what he'd like to do when he grows up. List them on paper, and suggest some other occupations. Then, together, do an internet search for each of these respective jobs, asking questions such as, "What's the average pay for a fast-food worker?" — or an accountant, an electrician, a doctor, or an engineer, etc. Explain that you are showing him these employment facts not to put anyone down but rather to highlight the potential difference in pay and benefits. The final portion of this lesson then is — whatever your son or grandson shows interest in —highlighting the educational requirements needed to do that job. And for many, this includes doing very well in high school to get into the schools to actually "do what they want to do," rather than "what they have to do," when they grow up.

Principle #7

Positive Attitude:
How You Think Is Everything

*"Whether you think you can, or think
you can't, you're right."*

— Henry Ford

THE POWER OF POSITIVE THINKING

JUST 30 DAYS after 9/11 2001, it happened;
the doctor told me that I "would live, but would
probably never walk again." One moment, while
serving my country overseas, I am healthy and
strong; the next I am being placed on a military
Blackhawk helicopter for emergency "life flight" to
a hospital in Germany. I now had a broken back,
my spinal cord was cut, and I was paralyzed from
the chest down for nine months. My life and that

of my young family were just turned upside down and changed forever.

But rather than blaming God, being negative, or believing my life was ruined, I chose to have a positive attitude. I believed that God still had more work for me to do while in the military. So, I remember telling the doctor, "You don't know me, and I don't know you, but I will walk again." And do you know what? By the grace of God, I did.

COURAGE, CONFIDENCE, AND ACCOMPLISHMENT – HAVING A "CAN DO, WILL DO" ATTITUDE

Although life at times includes the valleys of sorrow and darkness, it likewise is filled with peaks of joy and sunshine. Everyone faces trials and difficulties in life; some obstacles are just more challenging for us to overcome. The key to remember is that you have a choice to stay down, or to rise up, to let fear and doubt make you negative, or to have courage and confidence to conquer it — how you think is everything.

Having a "can do, will do," positive attitude leads to having the courage and confidence for you to act, face your fear or obstacle head-on, and just do it. Dale Carnegie said, "Inaction breeds doubt and fear. Action breeds confidence and courage.

If you want to conquer fear, do not sit home and think about it. Go out and get busy." Success breeds success — meaning, when you succeed at one thing, you then have the confidence and courage to succeed at other things.

BEING A LEADER AND A GOOD FOLLOWER

Volumes of books are written about being a good leader, but it is just as important to be a good follower. Why? Because, throughout your life, you will need to follow others, such as parents, grandparents, teachers, mentors, boss at work, etc. Being a good leader and a good follower requires a positive attitude. For an example, say your parents desire the very best for you, and they assign you very specific daily and weekly chores around the house for you to accomplish. You have a choice: you can — and should — have the love and respect for your parent/parents to do each chore or job and do it well. That's being responsible; that's because you have a good, positive attitude.

Now, can you imagine if you decided that you just didn't want to make your bed, take out the trash, set the table, or mow the lawn? After all, you're too busy playing your video game, watching TV, or texting your friends. Perhaps your parents constantly have to remind you of your responsibilities. This is a good example of having a bad attitude. So what's the big deal? This little stuff isn't important — or is it? Yes, it is, as your "attitude" will determine your "altitude" — or in other words, how high you can go. No one enjoys being around a negative person with a negative attitude. So learn now to be a responsible, decisive, proactive leader and follower with a positive attitude and respect for others.

SELF-TALK – THE MOST IMPORTANT CONVERSATION YOU'LL HAVE IS WITH YOURSELF

It is good when a gentleman recognizes when he has made a mistake and then corrects it. However, it is not good to continually put yourself down or be negative about yourself and others. Self-talk — or the way you choose to think and speak about yourself — is *your choice.*

Doe Zantamata said it this way: "Tell yourself, everything will work out. Things will get better. You are important. You are worthy of great things. You are loveable. The time is now. This too shall pass. You can be who you really are. The best is yet to come. You are strong. You can do this." This is sound wisdom and advice, to constantly be positive and tell yourself you can do it. Regardless of the obstacles in your way or negative people who say you can't. Remember, it is your life, and the decision is yours — choose to have a positive attitude, and life's doors and windows of opportunity will open to you.

Your Attitude, Positive Or Negative, Will Determine Your Day, Month, Year, And Life—Choose Wisely

For Parents, Grandparents, and Mentors

◆ **The Point:**

There is power in positive thinking — it builds courage and confidence, which, in turn, establishes a "can do, will do" attitude, which is vital in navigating through the challenges and trials of life. The real question is not *if* we will face these obstacles and challenges throughout our life but rather *how* we will handle them. The key to remember is that you have a choice to stay down or to rise up, to let fear and doubt make you negative, or to have the courage and confidence to conquer it — how you think is everything. Likewise, preparing your son(s) or grandson(s) to tackle life's challenges head-on is your responsibility, and this includes him having a positive attitude.

◆ **Studies Show:**

According to the Mayo Clinic (2017), "Researchers continue to explore the effects of positive thinking and optimism on health. Health benefits that positive thinking may provide include:

• Increased lifespan

• Lower rates of depression

- Lower rates of distress
- Greater resistance to the common cold
- Better psychological and physical well-being
- Better cardiovascular health and reduced risk of death from cardiovascular disease
- Better coping skills during hardships and times of stress."

Parents and grandparents, if these and other studies highlight such significant "health benefits" of positive thinking, then isn't it logical that you make it a priority to actively teach your son(s) and grandson(s) the vital importance of having a positive attitude? As always, teaching them a lesson is good, but showing them through your example is even better.

- **Lesson/Activity:**
  It's Movie Time! Parents and grandparents, here's a fun night to enjoy with your family, but especially to reinforce your son or grandson's grasp on the importance of having a positive attitude and the consequences of his choices. Depending upon his age (appropriate), here are a few top recommendations:

* *Forever Strong* PG-13, Rugby Sports, Drama (93% Google users liked this movie)

* *Courageous* PG-13 Personal Tragedy, Priorities and Faith (87% liked this movie)

* *The Lion King* G Courage, Responsibility, Strength, and Love (93% liked this movie)

* *Ratatouille* G Fantasy/Coming of Age (95% liked this movie)

After watching the movie together, take some time afterward to discuss some of the main points or lessons. Be certain to ask your son or grandson some open-ended questions that reinforce the principle of having a positive attitude. And finally, extend your own attitude of gratitude to him for the areas he personally does very well. Your honest and sincere praise will help reinforce his personal self-esteem and promote further acts of positive thinking.

Principle #8

Priorities: First Things First, What's Most Important

"Decide what you want, decide what you are willing to exchange for it. Establish your priorities and go to work."

— H. L. Hunt

WHAT'S YOUR IDEA OF SUCCESS?

THE HOLLYWOOD movies, magazines, internet, TV, billboards, and music of today would have you believe that a successful man drives an Italian sports car, has no inclination for marriage and children, dates only unrealistic gorgeous super-models, lives in a mansion on the ocean, and enjoys a never-ending surplus of money! Think James Bond, 007. Guess what? James Bond is a fictitious character (he's not real), and if he were real, after just a couple weeks of "007 fun," he'd be terribly unhappy, alone, and most likely be dead.

WHAT DO YOU WANT?

Earlier we related the options of "good, better, or best" in deciding upon your own character. As you strive for excellence in your life, some things are just more important than others — these are "priorities." This is really important, because what you want or desire will determine your priorities. Dallin H. Oaks said it this way: "Desires dictate our priorities, priorities shape our choices, and choices determine our actions." Therefore, decide what you want, what's most important — not just good or better, but the very best. Establish how you're going to do it, and then do it. Always remember who you are and that others' "priorities," or their idea of being "the best" and/or "successful" may not actually be the best, or even good.

FOCUS ON THE BIG ROCKS FIRST

A teacher is doing an experiment in his class. He fills a clear glass jar with big rocks and then asks the class if it's full. The class responds with a loud

"Yes." Then, the teacher adds some pebbles to the jar. He asks again if the jar is full, and again the class responds, "Yes." The teacher then adds some sand to the jar. Before asking if the jar is full, he reaches under the table and pours water into the jar. The teacher says, "The jar is now completely full," and the class learns a valuable lesson on priorities.

He said the "jar" represents time; the "big rocks" represent our most-important things in life, while the "pebbles, sand, and water" represent the other, smaller, less-important things. If we don't fit the "big rocks" (most important things) into the jar (our time) "first," our lives will be filled only with pebbles, sand, and water (less-important things), as the big rocks will not fit. We all have exactly the same 24 hours each day, but what and how you choose to fill your time — well, that's determined by your "priorities."

SELFLESSNESS VERSUS SELFISHNESS

It is vitally important for a man to take charge of his life, set goals and priorities, and then go out and accomplish them. It is likewise important to make a top priority of serving and helping others. This is being *selfless*. A great example of serving and sacrifice is found deep within the lives, and, yes, priorities, of America's founding fathers. On July 3, 1776, John Adams, who later became the second President of the United States, wrote a letter to his wife, Abigail, saying, "... I am well aware of the toil and blood and treasure that it will cost us to maintain this declaration, and support and defend these states. Yet, through all the gloom, I can see the rays of ravishing light and glory. I can see that the end is more than worth the means ..." This man's inspiring words remind us of our most-important priorities and our solemn responsibility to others. Are we willing to pay the price?

In our day, there are those around us who provide selfless acts of service in countless ways. For instance, I have a dear friend who has provided me with an extraordinary example of being selfless through his acts of kindness and service to others. Although many of his actions appear to be random, I have learned that he has made it his priority to deliberately plan and serve others. Here's just one example. On my birthday, every year, without fail, he calls me and wishes me a happy birthday. He does the same for my wife. He does the same for my children. Now get this, he does the same for every man, woman, and child in our church congregation of hundreds of people and hundreds more.

Now, your first impression is perhaps something like, "Well, that's nice, but he's obviously got a lot of time to make all these calls — right?" Wrong. He's an extremely busy man with his own wife and children, and a professional career as vice president of a large bank. He volunteers countless hours serving in his community. So how does he do it? It's actually less random and very much a deliberately planned and organized service to others. Why? Because he's made it a lifetime priority of deciding what's most important.

Your Desires Dictate Priorities, Priorities Shape Choices, Choices Determine Your Actions

For Parents, Grandparents, and Mentors

◆ **The Point:**
Priorities. Put plainly and right to the point:

*"No other success can compensate
for failure in the home."*

— David O. McKay

Home — a sanctuary from the world. A place of love, order, learning, and building lasting family relationships.

Your legacy — what you create, what impact you've made, what you leave behind.

◆ **Studies Show:**
According to *Inc.* (2018), "Science says 92 percent of people don't achieve their goals. Here's how the other 8 percent do ... consistently and exceptionally well ... setting specific and challenging goals. Basically, the more specific and challenging your goals, the higher your motivation toward hitting them."

Forbes (2014) published research on priorities and the importance of actually writing down your goals. Their findings provided four clear and measurable steps that lead to huge success:

1) *Create a Vision* — Prioritize what you want (most important); what does your ideal life look like? You get to dream.

2) *Make It Measurable* — Take your vision, and make a list of your goals to get there.

3) *Set Benchmarks* — Break your goals into small, actionable steps, and assign a time-frame for completing each one.

4) *Celebrate Your Success* — Reward yourself for hitting your benchmarks and reaching your goals.

◆ Lesson/Activity:

Focus on the Big Rocks First. Here's a fun-to-do activity that you can easily do with your son(s) and/or grandson(s) that will make a lasting impression concerning his own priorities. First, go to the "Big Rocks" section of this chapter, and either:

a) Read it out loud together, or

b) Actually do the experiment together, hands-on. Be sure to reinforce this lesson by reversing the order by starting with the water, sand, and pebbles (the small stuff) first. Then he will see that the big rocks (the most-important things) will not fit into the jar (time) after the water, sand, and pebbles. Note to fathers and grandfathers: unlike a pinewood derby car, it's actually better to let *him* do it, rather than just watch from a distance.

After you do the aforementioned experiment, here's one more quick lesson to make this chapter on priorities even more personal.

Step #1: Preplanning — Write the following either on your computer or on a piece of paper:

"MY PRIORITIES, MY CHOICES, MY LIFE"
Decide *what you want*, what's *most important*, not just good, or better, but *the very best*; establish *how you're going to do it* and then *do it*.

1. **What's Most Important (List my Top 3 Priorities):**

    a) _____

    b) _____

    c) _____

2. **How Do I Spend Most of My Time?**

    a) _____

    b) _____

    c) _____

3. **What Changes am I Willing to Make in Order to Accomplish My Priorities?**

    a) _____

    b) _____

    c) _____

4. **Set a Specific Date for Achieving Each of My Top Priorities and Measure My Progress Along the Way:**

    Priority #1: _____ **By this Date:** _____

    Measure: (Start ---------------X --------------**Finished)**

    Priority #2: _____ **By this Date:** _____

    Measure: (Start ---------------X --------------**Finished)**

    Priority #3: _____ **By this Date:** _____

    Measure: (Start ---------------X --------------**Finished)**

Step #2: Doing it — Have your son(s) and/ or grandson(s) fill out their own list. When it's complete, place it where they can see it often and update their progress as they move toward their goals and gain confidence. This activity will teach him a vital life lesson in determining his top priorities — his choices of what's most important, not just good or better, but the very best — and in establishing how he's going to do it and then actually doing it.

Principle #9

Learn the Value of Hard Work

"Winners embrace hard work. They love the discipline of it, the trade-off they're making to win. Losers, on the other hand, see it as a punishment. And that's the difference."

— Lou Holtz

BEWARE OF EASY

STANLEY ELLIS suggests, "Be careful with easy … hard is good." He explains, "In the world of nature, hard is part of the circle of life. It is hard for a baby chick to hatch out of that tough eggshell. But when someone tries to make it easier, the chick does not develop the strength necessary to live. In a similar way, the struggle of a butterfly to escape the cocoon strengthens it for the life it will live" (2017). Likewise, throughout your entire

79

life, you should beware of easy, of having the expectation that everyone owes you something or that everything should be somehow handed to you. It is vitally important that you learn the value of hard work. Do not avoid it. Embrace it. You will become not only the man you *want* to be but the man you're actually *willing* to be, through your hard work.

> *"All life demands struggle. Those who have everything given to them become lazy, selfish, and insensitive to the real values of life. The very striving and hard work that we so constantly try to avoid is the major building block in the person we are today."*
>
> — Pope Paul VI

THERE'S A TIME FOR WORK AND A TIME FOR PLAY—KNOW THE DIFFERENCE

Why? Because when you grow up, you'll be expected to already know how to work hard in order to get a good job, which means doing well in school, going to college to get more school, and being responsible and respectable. Although you'll have time to play and should, there are no shortcuts, as hard work is a foundational corner-stone to success. Now, if all you do growing up is play video games non-stop and watch movies, life — not your "virtual life" where you're "master of the universe," but your real life — will most likely be very disappointing with how things turn out. It's not as easy as seeing "Game Over" and simply hitting the "Start Over" button. In other words, the real game of life requires hard work and rewards those who do it.

DETERMINATION, PERSISTENCE, AND OVERCOMING OBSTACLES

As a young man and throughout your life, you will experience obstacles along the way; you'll make mistakes and experience failure. These challenges may be physical, mental, emotional, and/or spiritual. The key is how you react when you're faced with these trials in life. Zig Ziglar said, "Failure is an event, not a person. Yesterday ended last night. Today is a brand new day ... and it's yours." It takes determination and persistence to overcome obstacles, also courage and wisdom to learn from your mistakes and to keep striving to do your best.

Chuck Norris once said, "I've always found that anything worth achieving will always have obstacles in the way, and you've got to have that drive and determination to overcome those obstacles en route to whatever it is that you want to accomplish." Some look for easy paths or simple ways to climb to the top. Yet, simple and easy will never lead you to the top of a mountain. So when you're at the foot of the mountain, faced with life's trials and obstacles, and the top looks very far away, remember this: hard work is not a guarantee against failure, but rather it develops the traits and discipline necessary to overcome it. So, as you climb that mountain, you may slide all the way back to the bottom several times, but through hard work, you will achieve the summit eventually and enjoy the reward of that majestic view — earned only by those who truly understand the merits of hard work and never give up.

"There are no secrets to success. It is the result of preparation, hard work, and learning from failure."

— Colin Powell

Success Follows Those Who Plan, Work Hard, And Never Give Up

For Parents, Grandparents, and Mentors

♦ ## The Point:

I recently listened to a conference where a man spoke of his days as a financial consultant. He said that most of his clients were multimillionaires who created and built their own business from nothing to a success through lots of hard work. He said the saddest part of his work was to hear many of them say that they wanted to make it easier for their children. They didn't want their children to have to suffer as they had. He said, in other words, they were depriving their children of the very thing (hard work) that had made them successful.

Just because you *can* give your children and grandchildren something does not mean that you *should*, let alone give them *everything*. Taking away their ability to learn the value of hard work is not helping them but rather setting them up for failure when they enter the "real world" on their own. Dave Ramsey said, "Teaching a child to work is not child abuse. We teach them to work not for our benefit but because it gives them both dignity in a job well done today and the tools and character to win in the future as adults."

◆ **Studies Show:**

Research consistently reveals the correlation between the "value of hard work" and "elite performers" over a wide range of fields. For example, there was a study of 20-year-old violinists who performed while a panel of teachers judged each and placed them into three separate groups in order to determine how much work each put into their instrument. Here's what they found:

- The "Good" group averaged 5,000 deliberate hours of practice over their lives.

- The "Better" group averaged 7,500 deliberate hours of practice over their lives.

- The "Best" group averaged 10,000 deliberate hours of practice over their lives.

It's the same story in surgery, insurance sales, and virtually every sport. The more deliberate practice (hard work), the better the performance. Tons of it (hard work) equals great performance. Finally, take basketball legend Michael Jordan as the ultimate in "natural talent" — right? Not likely, as he was cut from his high school basketball team. Yet, throughout Jordan's career, he practiced intensely above and beyond the brutal practice routines and became great, even legendary (*Fortune*, 2006).

> *"Some people want it to happen; some wish it would happen; others make it happen."*
>
> — Michael Jordan

◆ **Lesson/Activity:**

Hard Work: Earn It — Then You'll Learn It. This lesson of learning the value of hard work is best taught not by your words alone but by your son(s) and/or grandson(s) step-by-step experience in actually "doing." Note: In order to instill a strong, positive work ethic, it's best to start early, as our habits become our character, and our character becomes our destiny.

Step #1: Teach him while he's young the difference between needs and wants and his expectations. For example, basic *needs* include food, water, shelter, love, a stable and safe living environment, physical exercise, education through learning, and structured discipline to name a few. His *wants* and *desires* may include a new cell phone, gizmos, and gadgets, candy, toys, designer sneakers, new TV, etc.

Step #2: When your son or grandson tells you they *want* something, rather than you just buying it for them, suggest to them a way of *earning it for themselves.* This lesson includes *their* (age-appropriate) hard work and the result, or reward, of them earning what they *want.* Some parents unwittingly make the mistake of spoiling their children, which deprives them of one of the greatest tools in life, which is to say, you get what you *earn* — not just because you *want* it.

Principle #10
Financial Management

"Wealth is largely the result of habit."

— John Jacob Astor

SO, YOU HAVE A JOB – NOW WHAT?

YOU'RE THE man! You've got a job, you're looking good, you're feeling good, you've got money in your pocket, and it's time to spend, spend, spend — right? No, no, no! If that's what you do, it will all be gone, gone, gone. Here's why: Regardless of how old you are, or how much you make, unless you know how to manage your money, your money will never be enough as it freely flows through your fingers like water. The good news, it doesn't have to be this way. You can decide where your money goes — before you spend it — and this means having a budget.

KNOW HOW TO BUDGET YOUR MONEY

Having a budget shows you what you can afford and likewise what you cannot afford, but without exercising restraint, a budget does not *keep you from buying it* — this requires discipline. Comedian Steve Martin said, "I love money. I love everything about it. I bought some pretty good stuff. Got me a $300 pair of socks. Got a fur sink. An electric dog polisher. A gasoline-powered turtleneck sweater. And, of course, I bought some dumb stuff, too."

Essentially, a budget is your personal "money plan." By creating and effectively using a budget, you plan how you will use your money for a certain period of time. For example, you'll first write down your "income" (how much you make); then, you'll keep track of and write down all of your "expenses" (where and how much you spend). As you put your budget together, you may find that you have more in expenses than income; if you do, you're not alone. That's where a budget comes in — to help show you that you really can't afford the "$300 pair of socks" or the "electric dog polisher." A budget, or, in other words, your money plan, is a great tool which helps you to "live within your means."

LIVING WITHIN YOUR MEANS

Once upon a time, long, long ago, there lived a very happily married couple. She was absolutely beautiful, and he was ruggedly handsome (but that's beside the point). Although they had very little money, their very first year together, they wanted desperately to make each other happy, so they each bought the other extravagant and expensive gifts. They rejoiced in their new higher standard of living for almost a full month — that is, until the bills came to them demanding payment. They quickly learned a most valuable and important life lesson about money — if you can't afford it, then don't buy it. To live within your means is to live in peace. In contrast, being in debt and not having the means to pay for it is like having a root canal without any pain medicine to numb your face, performed by your Uncle Merlin, who is not a dentist! I know, because long, long ago, I was ruggedly handsome.

SAVING AND INVESTING

Here's a universal truth: "Ready or not, your future is coming." So, how do you see yourself 5, 10, 20, or even 40 years from now? I suspect most people dream of a happy, comfortable, safe, and bright future; but a dream without a plan to get there is only a wish. The real question is: Are you willing to pay the price to create the life you want for you and your family? Mega-millionaire Malcolm Forbes once said, "I made my money the old-fashioned way. I was very nice to a wealthy relative right before he died." Yet, for almost everyone else, this means saving and investing.

Basic, general examples of saving and investing include:

- *An Emergency Fund* — Save one to six months of your income for an emergency fund, as unexpected things happen. But use it for only worst-case situations, e.g., your car breaks down, you get laid off of work, etc. (new shoes don't count).

- *Eliminate Debt* — Saving extra money each month to pay off debt is critically important. Then, avoid consumer debt (credit cards, etc.) like the plague or brussels sprouts.

- *Home Ownership* — Buying a home is another way to invest, but it may not be right for everyone. Buy a home when and where it makes sense for you, and buy only what you can comfortably afford — this means living within your means.

- *Education* — Investing in yourself is wise, but remember Principle #6 on education:

Invest only in a field of study or training that will lead you to better work and pay.

– *Retirement Account* — This is an investment in your and your family's future.

Here's a quick quiz on investing: Assuming you earn 8 percent compound interest on your investments, who do you think will make the most in the following scenarios?

#1 Scenario: You invest $300 each month beginning at age 25.

#2 Scenario: Your friend Roger invests $600 each month beginning at age 35.

#3 Scenario: Your other friend Kevin invests $1,200 each month beginning at age 45.

Here are the results at age 65 for you and your other two friends:

"You" at just $300 each month made the most at $1,010,812—yep, $1 million!

– Next is Roger at $600 each month. He waited until he was 35 and made $888,090.

– Last is Kevin at $1,200 each month. He waited until he was 45 and made $726,090.

The moral of this story is "You're Rich!" No, seriously: the lesson is really to "Start Young." The earlier, the better. Yet, as you can see from the example, it is better to begin as soon as you can, even if it is later, rather than not beginning to save and invest at all.

There is one final moral in this exercise. It is that *money does not buy happiness.* There are many rich people in the world who are not happy. One of the greatest blessings of life is to continue to give, to lift up the poor, and to bless the lives of others. When you understand the simple phrase, "Because I have been given much, I, too, must give," you understand the true meaning of wealth and happiness.

> *Obtaining Wealth Is Easy: Spend Less Than You Earn, Stay Out Of Debt, Save, Invest, And Give Regularly*

For Parents, Grandparents, and Mentors

◆ **The Point:**

One of the greatest gifts you can ever give your son and/or grandson is to teach him sound financial-management principles. Those who hope or assume he will learn all of this money stuff in school or perhaps just figures it out on his own risk too much — and the consequences could be devastating. Let's face it: his financial management "IQ" will most likely influence not only his own quality of life but also the quality of life for his spouse, children, grandchildren, etc. Just as in building a home, a sure and steady foundation must be set first, before you can erect a structure made to weather the storms and last. Likewise, your son and/or grandson must have a firm "financial" foundation in order to stand strong and weather the storms of life.

◆ **Studies Show:**

In a CNBC article (2016), U.S. schools get a failing grade for financial-literacy education. *"Exposure is everything ... when you learn good habits, you tend to have better outcomes."* Morrison (2016), of the Council for Economic Education said, *"Apart from age and inexperience, adolescents in the U.S. lack basic personal finance skills because they receive little coaching at home ... that sets them up for failure in the years immediately following high school graduation."*

In a global study of nearly 30,000 teenagers from 18 countries, *"more than 1 in 6 students in the U.S. failed to reach the baseline level of proficiency in financial literacy ... overall, American students fall in the middle of the pack globally, performing on average just behind Latvia and just ahead of Russia."* Paris-based Organization for Economic Co-operation and Development (2012).

◆ **Lesson/Activity:**

Finance 101. Depending upon the age of your son and/or grandson, select one of the following lessons/activities to do together. Due to the criticality of him not only learning about financial matters but also actually doing, you may want to select a date and time each week for several weeks in a row in order to ensure he truly "gets it" and then continually follow up to reinforce the lesson.

  ◦ *Making a Budget* — Regardless of his age, together create a budget with his income and his expenses. This is a perfect time to reinforce "living within his means" and "staying out of debt."

- *Save* — If he's young, there's nothing like having *him* save in his own "piggy bank" or jar.

- *Opening a Savings Account* — Teach why it's necessary; then go and do it.

- *Opening a Checking Account* — Teach why and how to balance; then go and do it.

- *Debit and/or Credit Cards* — Teach about them, various interest rates, and debt.

- *Mutual Funds, Stocks, Bonds* — Teach about them, various risks vs. reward, fees, etc.

- *Real Estate* — Teach about investing in and/ or home ownership vs. renting.

- The Gift of Giving — Teach him to set aside a portion of his income to bless others.

As in all lessons, your own personal example is vitally important, and the time you spend now to teach will surely pay dividends for your family in the future.

Principle #11

Health and Fitness:
Mind, Body, and Spirit

"Self-discipline is the triumph over the chains of self-gratification."

— Being Caballero

BEYOND VIDEO GAMES AND TV – WHAT ELSE IS THERE IN LIFE?

HAVE YOU ever seen the TV commercials advertising a new prescription-drug medicine? They often make such huge claims about how you'll be so much healthier and happier; they show people literally walking through a field of flowers. Meanwhile, a voice in the background is rapidly reading (and oftentimes microscopic-sized print at the bottom of the screen) is listing a legal disclaimer, or warning, such as:

> "*If you feel dizziness, headaches, blurred vision, upset stomach, blotchy skin, pelvic discomfort, etc., STOP taking this medication, and call a doctor immediately. You may be suffering from side effects, and the result may lead to a stroke, heart attack, blindness, or death.*"

Wow! That's an example of *Buy this — it will make you happy, yet the consequences for some are really bad.* This is true with most anything, but how can playing video games, which is fun and makes you happy, have consequences? Like eating peanut butter, probably nothing, but eat a jar a day and, most likely, you'll have consequences. Here's what the experts say — about excess video gaming, not peanut butter:

– Excessive video gaming on a portable unit, television, or the internet can affect your life.

– Limit yourself to no more than two hours of screen time per day (playing games, TV, and internet).

– Video-game addiction can be as bad as gambling and may start as early as 8 years old.

– A sign of addiction may be if you constantly think about your next video-game session, devise ways to get back to the game, stop former hobbies that don't relate to video games, or decline social events with real people because you'd rather spend time in your virtual world.

– If you spend all your free time playing video games and skipping meals or deprive yourself of sleep due to excessive play, it can create health problems, including headaches, backaches, eyestrain, obesity, etc.

– Other potential issues include jeopardized relationships, increased aggression, poor performance in school, etc.

— The Negative Effects of Video Game Addiction (2017)

So what's a guy to do? Part of growing up is being responsible. The idea of someone living in their parents' basement at 40 because they cannot get a job because their only skill set is "expert video gamer" (by choice) is hardly responsible. It's downright lazy, selfish, and sad. The good news is that you have lots of choices. Learning and participating in sports, music, reading good books (such as the one in your hand), and various other hobbies will expand your mind. If you're engaged in sports, you will also improve your overall health, strength, and fitness.

HOBBIES, SPORTS, AND EXTRACURRICULAR ACTIVITIES

Have you ever:

- Climbed a mountain, finally reached the top of the summit, and then experienced the exhilarating sense of accomplishment while taking in the breathtaking views and feeling like you're on top of the world?

- Played sports on a team and, in the final seconds, hit the winning basket? Scored the winning touchdown? Hit in the winning run? Kicked the winning goal, etc. and then experienced the thrill of winning, accomplishment, competition, and, likewise, the importance of learning teamwork?

- Spent time in the great outdoors hunting, fishing, boating, sailing, water skiing, snow skiing, golfing, swimming, surfing, scuba diving, or traveled to other states or countries to enjoy the wonderful diversity of people, cultures, foods and lifestyles?

If you answered "Yes" to any of the aforementioned, then you already know the amazing experiences that come to those who do them. If you have not, a whole new world is out there, waiting for you to enjoy. This is being well-rounded and living a balanced life.

BALANCE AND OVERALL WELL-BEING – PHYSICAL, MENTAL, EMOTIONAL, AND SPIRITUAL

"That's enough!" exclaimed my wife, after watching me press 600 pounds (twice) in a military weight-lifting challenge. In contrast, it was only six years earlier, shortly after suffering a broken back and serious spinal cord injury, my loving wife whispered to me, "That's enough" as she watched me struggle in lifting just the 40-pound bar with no weights. A lot happened from that difficult day to get me to a much better, happier, and healthy day six years later. Here are some key highlights that really helped me and likewise might help you, too:

– *Spiritual* — Have faith, pray, develop a relationship with God, a higher being or a belief in something bigger then ourselves will strengthen us in ways that man cannot explain.

- *Mental and Emotional* — Your attitude and mental toughness are critical when you find that you're at the foot of the mountain, and the climb seems so difficult and the top so very far away. Every journey begins with the first step — be positive, have courage, and take it!

- *Physical* — Nothing takes the place of hard work. It requires grit, determination, and sacrifice. If you want to build muscles, you must work them, train them, eat nutritionally, and then rest them.

It is not an accident that each of the chapters of this book discusses key principles such as: vision, character, having a positive attitude, determination, hard work, education, health and fitness, etc. Each are essential "life skills" to ensure you have the fundamental tools to succeed and find a healthy balance in your life — mind, body, and spirit.

BEWARE OF THE CHAINS OF ADDICTION

Everyone makes mistakes, but to repeat this behavior over and over is dangerous. Just like the earlier chapter on "Choosing Your Friends Wisely," you must be aware of those people around you who try to influence your life in making bad choices. What may seem to be harmless, like smoking a cigarette, drinking alcohol, viewing pornography, or trying drugs, may later take away your freedom and bind you in the chains of addiction. If you are wondering if this is really true, simply talk with someone who smokes several packs of cigarettes a day — they will most likely tell you that it is expensive, that it is greatly affecting their health in a very bad way, and that they wished they'd never smoked their first cigarette — because they're now addicted, and it's very hard to stop.

"THE WOLVES WITHIN" – A CHEROKEE LEGEND

An old grandfather said to his grandson, who came to him with anger at a friend who had done him an injustice, "Let me tell you a story. I, too, at times, have felt a great hate for those who have taken so much, with no sorrow for what they do. But hate wears you down and does not hurt your enemy. It is like taking poison and wishing your enemy would die. I have struggled with these feelings many times." He continued, "It is as if there are two wolves inside me. One is good and does no harm. He lives in harmony with all around him and does not take offense when no offense was intended. He will fight only when it is right to do so, and in the right way.

"But the other wolf — ah! He is full of anger. The smallest thing will set him into a fit of temper. He fights everyone, all the time, for no reason. He cannot think because his anger and hate are so great. It is helpless anger, for his anger will change nothing. Sometimes it is hard to live with these two wolves inside me, for both of them try to dominate my spirit."

The boy looked intently into his grandfather's eyes and asked, "Which one wins, grandfather?"

The grandfather smiled and quietly said, "The one I feed."

True Strength Requires A Self-Disciplined Mind, Body, And Spirit

For Parents, Grandparents, and Mentors

◆ **The Point:**

Technology is great. It is incredible just how much better our lives can be because of it — right? Well, it depends on how it's used. Far too many children, especially boys, are so consumed with playing video games, watching TV, and/or being on social media constantly that they're living in a virtual world. It is imperative for young men to be physically, mentally, morally fit and healthy. There's no comparison between a young man who's outdoors, or on a court playing sports in the real world, versus someone else sitting in a dark room alone pushing buttons and/or a joystick on a console in the virtual world. You must ensure that he has ample opportunities to actively cultivate his mind, body, and spirit. After all, his health, good or bad, will be a direct reflection of his daily habits.

◆ **Studies Show:**

According to the U.S. Centers for Disease Control (2017), *"Regular physical activity in childhood and adolescence is important for promoting lifelong health and well-being and preventing various health conditions.*" Their guidelines recommend that children and adolescents aged 6 to 17 years should have at least 60 minutes or more of physical activity each day. Unfortunately, only 21.6% of young people attained 60 or more minutes of moderate to vigorous physical activity at least 5 days per week.

The CDC lists these benefits of physical activity:

Regular physical activity can help children and adolescents improve cardiorespiratory fitness, build strong bones and muscles, control weight, reduce symptoms of anxiety and depression, and reduce the risk of developing health conditions such as:

* Heart Disease
* Cancer
* Type 2 Diabetes
* High Blood Pressure
* Osteoporosis
* Obesity

The World Health Organization (2017) states, *"Less and less physical activity is occurring in many countries. Globally, 23% of adults and 81%*

school-going adolescents are not active enough." They reaffirm that a lack of physical activity is a significant risk factor for noncommunicable diseases such as stroke, diabetes, and cancer.

◆ **Lesson/Activity:**

The New Active, Happier, Healthier — More Than a New Year's Resolution in January That Ends in February — You (and Your Son)! Yes, spend some time with your son and/or grandson, and select a new sport and/or physical activity that you two can do together. The options and opportunities are near limitless. You might even consider making a list and trying new activities each week until you find his niche that gets him and you excited to go again and again. The lessons in doing these activities together are vitally important for his (and your) health — and the time shared together is truly priceless.

"My priority is to turn people — especially kids — on to sports and being active so they don't even have to think about it being good for their health. If people participate for the fun of it — and believe me, it is fun — then fitness programs will be much more successful."

— Alan Thicke

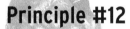

Principle #12

The Most Important Decision of Your Life

*"Don't marry the person you think you
can live with; marry only the individual
you think you can't live without."*

— James Dobson

DATING – AND AT THE RIGHT TIME,
THE RIGHT PERSON – MARRIAGE

A GENTLEMAN knows the difference between just hanging out with his friends and going on a proper date. If you want to impress a prospective date, then you'll first have to have the courage to ask them out on a date. This means that you probably should have some idea in advance of what it is you'd like to do together and already have a proposed date and time. Note: a wise man will consider their date's interests and not assume they'll enjoy a 4-hour mud tractor pull! A gentleman will remember the earlier principles discussed in this book and that dressing appropriately, personal hygiene, manners, etc. are top priorities. A gentleman will be punctual (pick their date up on time). If you're meeting their parents, remember the section on handshakes, looking into the eyes of the person, and, speaking clearly, say something like, "It is a pleasure to meet you, Mr. Smith." But only if his name is "Smith," otherwise, it may be a very short date.

A gentleman always pays for the expenses of the date. Asking someone on a date and then asking them to pay their own way, or worse, asking them to pay for both of you is a sure way to earn a "cheap" reputation. But a word of caution: You need not get into debt trying to impress anyone. It is likewise important that you stick to your financial goals, and that includes living within your means. Group dates are also an option if you'd feel more comfortable with another couple. Always remember, a gentleman respects everyone especially women, all women, young and old, and treats each with dignity and respect. After your date, it is always proper for you to call them the following day and express your appreciation for a fun time at the zoo, the movie, the dance, etc. It's the right thing to do and shows respect, regardless of whether you'll ask them out on another date again or not.

Now, after many years of dating many different people, you may find someone who takes your breath away, who makes you laugh, who is just a part of you, and you want to spend all your time with them. In other words, you'll know — at the right time, at the right place, and with especially the right person — that you will be making the most important decision of your life — marriage.

> *"If you want to know how your girl will treat you after marriage, just listen to her talking to her little brother."*
>
> — Sam Levenson

THE PROPOSAL

When the time comes that you've finally found the love of your life, your best friend, the future partner to help raise your children — the one for you — *do not* casually mention to them that you've been thinking about getting married, and, well, "How about it?" No, here are a few suggestions to make this sacred event much more special — especially for your future spouse:

– Before asking your future spouse to marry you, you should respectfully ask their father for his blessing, or their mother's blessing, as appropriate. Why? Because you will be marrying into their family, and good relations with the family are important, as they'll be the grandparents to your future children. Aunts, uncles, nieces, nephews come as a new blessing, too.

– Plan something special. Think of something that they'll always remember and cherish. Make it a romantic setting, like at a sunset, near the ocean, lakefront, or a waterfall, etc. If you play an instrument, other than tuba, you might consider writing them a love song and playing it, or hire a professional, or a perfectly timed fireworks display.

– Purchase a ring (one you can afford and *return* if they desire a different style, or *man*).

– Dress for the occasion — this is a very special day. Make it memorable in every way.

– At the perfect moment, before proposing, share your own personal feelings about *why* you love them and *how much* you desire to spend forever with them. Then, be certain to drop to one knee, pulling the ring from your pocket. Open the ring box, and call them by name. While looking into the beautiful eyes of the one you love, lovingly and sincerely ask if they will do you the great honor and privilege of marrying you!

Or, you may casually mention that you've been thinking about getting married, and well, "How about it?" It's your choice, but hopefully, you can see the difference, because they most certainly will.

MARRIAGE

It's best to let your new fiancée plan your wedding. Most have dreamed of this special day, and they want it to be perfect — you should, too. However, some say a diamond is forever, and, like the wedding, the bigger the better. Yet it is wisdom to remember this ancient Chinese secret: "Big ring, big wedding ceremony, bring no more happiness. If you cannot afford and they don't care — you run, grasshopper, run!"

Okay, okay, it's not technically an ancient Chinese secret, but my recent DNA test shows that I do have 1% Asian ancestry (possibly Chinese), and I am getting older (some would call ancient) and perhaps wiser (otherwise one who knows great secrets). The point is, does this "ring" true? Yes, regardless of what all the media suggests, new research shows that a bigger diamond ring and/or an expensive wedding does not bring more happiness but more divorce — 3.5 times more. This is not to criticize those who can afford an expensive ring and wedding ceremony but rather to highlight the universal truth that money and expensive stuff does not buy happiness. It's always best to simply live within your means and remember that debt brings stress — and stress is something grasshoppers don't enjoy!

Marriage, to the right person, is like a slice of heaven on earth, but marriage to the wrong person, well, comedian Bill Murray said, "The fact that there's a highway to hell and only a stairway to heaven says a lot about anticipated traffic numbers." While another comedian, Rodney Dangerfield, said, "It's tough to stay married. My wife kisses the dog on the lips, yet she won't drink from my glass."

A key to a successful, happy marriage is to be selfless, not selfish. Give yourself to your spouse with complete fidelity and be faithful, honest, and trustworthy — be someone they can count on. Forgiveness is vital, and we all make mistakes. When you're wrong, admit it and apologize. When your spouse is wrong, be slow to criticize. Marriage is truly where your heart is; it's where your combined story begins. It's exciting and fun, and your courtship should not end with marriage. You should continue to go out on regular dates and keep the romance alive — especially important after you're blessed with children. Remember, the stairway to heaven requires climbing — in other words, it takes work, effort, and a daily commitment to each other to keep on climbing together — always together.

BECOMING "THAT KIND OF MAN"

"We need to teach our daughters to distinguish between:
A man who flatters her and a man who compliments her,
A man who spends money on her and a man who invests
in her,
A man who views her as property and a man who views
her properly,
A man who lusts after her and a man who loves her,
A man who believes he's a gift to women and a man who
believes she's a gift to him.
And then we need to teach our sons to be that kind of man."

— Unknown

It's up to you. The decision is entirely yours to make. Regardless of your individual circumstances — where you live, your race, your religion, your age, your height, your weight, your family's social status, rich or poor — you can become "That Kind of Man." Then, when you do, you will find the true meaning of success and happiness.

> *Becoming A Man Is Not About Finding Yourself, But Creating Yourself*

For Parents, Grandparents, and Mentors

◆ **The Point:**
Although this book has 12 essential life skills/
principles, there is one theme that is deliberately woven into the tapestry of each chapter,
and that is "time." Success is spelled T.I.M.E.
The more time you spend with your son and/or
grandson, the more he will learn from you and
grow. When you make a promise, keep it. He
will know that he is loved, that, even when he
makes mistakes — and he will — you are always
there for him. Fathers and grandfathers, your
example, such as how you treat your spouse,
by putting their needs above your own, will
greatly influence his behavior when he marries.

In closing, teach him, by spending time showing him the 12 essential life skills presented
in this book. Ensure that he knows them all in
order to become "That Kind of Man" — who
respects and honors others. In order for this
to happen and in the proper season of his life,
he must know how to go on a "proper date"
and how to respectfully treat that date. He
must know how to choose the "right" spouse
in marriage. He must know how a gentleman
proposes and be prepared in order to have a

successful marriage. Teach him these things, and the probability of him being "That Kind of Man" dramatically increases, not only for him, but for his children, and then his grandchildren … and the legacy continues...

> *"Most kids just follow the cycle. My grandfather didn't finish high school. My father didn't, and I didn't. But you can break the cycle. You can have a successful marriage and be a good father."*
>
> — Eric Thomas

◆ **Studies Show:**
In a multitude of research, Focus on the Family (2018) shares the following statistics on *The Significance of a Father's Influence:*

- *82% of studies on father involvement and child well-being published since 1980 found "significant associations between positive father involvement and offspring well-being …"*

- *In the words of Dr. Pruett, "Positive father care is associated with more pro-social and positive moral behavior in boys and girls. This is borne out by research from the University of Pennsylvania which indicates that children who feel a closeness and warmth with their father are twice as likely to enter college, 75% less likely to have a child in their teen years, 80% less likely to be incarcerated, and half as likely to show various signs of depression."*

◆ **Lesson/Activity:**

Dating 101—Get Specific. Similar to the absolute necessity of you having the "Birds and the Bees" talk, it is likewise essential for you to ensure that he's prepared for the emotional, physical, and spiritual elements of dating. Remember, this is your job, your responsibility. Otherwise, without a firm foundation, your son will be left to the influences of the internet, TV, magazines, social media, peer pressure, such as this marital advice:

"Some people ask the secret of our long marriage. We take time to go to a restaurant two times a week. A little candlelight, dinner, soft music, and dancing. She goes Tuesdays; I go Fridays."

— Henny Youngman

See what I mean? Now, depending on his age, here's some suggested dating topics:

– *Respect for your Date* — They are your equal; independent, capable and deserve your respect.

– *Manners and Etiquette* — Reference Principle #3.

– *Dress and Appearance* — Reference Principle #4.

– *Always a Gentleman* — No need for being the "Macho Man" and never the high school locker-room mentality of derogatory remarks about your date to your friends. A gentleman *never* discusses such things with his friends.

– *Value of Moral Behavior* — Respect, integrity, honesty, loyalty, courtesy, kindness, and humility still count, for you and for your date.

– *Boundaries* — Decide well in advance what is appropriate and what is not. Getting a girl pregnant and raising a child is a huge responsibility. It is always best to wait until you're in love, married, and have a good job, a place to live, etc., before you start a family.

– *Friendship Before Courtship* — It's much better to really know the values, morals, interests, etc., of your prospective date before deciding to go steady (meaning that you date exclusively with one another).

– *Going Steady* — Unless you're engaged to be married, continue to date others. You'll really want to know if they are the one. For example, if as a young kid, you've always liked vanilla ice cream, so that's all you ever try, you'll never know when you grow up and mature that you may really love Rocky Road or Butter Pecan.

– *Really Get to Know your Date* — Pretty is nice, but their heart is far more important. Emotional, intellectual, and spiritual matter far more than simply physical attraction.

– *Be Very Selective* — Those you decide to date will be those you will someday choose from to become your spouse, your best friend, and nurturer to your future children. It is *the most important decision of your life*, and it all begins with dating.

– *Always Remember Who You Are* — You represent not only yourself but your entire family as well as your family name. Those are things to be proud of.

If you're successful, your son or grandson will not only *act* like a gentleman around others —he'll actually *be* one! You will share in the journey and blessings of him "Becoming That Kind of Man."

About the Author

Dr. Rex S. Vanderwood is an internationally-recognized leader, speaker, and humanitarian, who for more than three decades, has impacted thousands of men, women, and children in more than forty countries worldwide. He served twenty-six years as a senior leader in the United States Air Force, eight years as a commander, responsible for $6.5 billion in Department of Defense assets and 38,000 people and their families.

Dr. Vanderwood has eight college degrees, including a doctorate in business administration, and is managing partner of a successful international strategic consulting firm. His global influence extends to international government leaders and organizations as diverse as the Vice President of the United States, South African Deputy President, Argentinian, Kyrgyzstan, and Slovenian heads of state to prestigious universities and colleges.

Dr. Vanderwood is the recipient of five Meritorious Service medals, the USAF's prestigious Lance P. Sijan Leadership Award, and the Excellence in Federal Government Leader of the Year Award. He was honored to receive the State of Hawaii's Joint Venture Education Forum's Top Contributor Award. Most importantly, he is a husband, son, father, and grandfather with a passion to help all people become their very best, and is the driving force behind this book.

Acknowledgments

THANK YOU to the countless parents, grandparents, and mentors across the world, who strive to make a difference, who serve and help others—especially children and young adults. You teach them, love them, build them up and lift them higher. You provide them with the essential life skills, or tools required for them to succeed in life.

Thank you to my dear father and mother—who through love and patience instilled the principles articulated in this book. My love and gratitude extends to my entire family, mentors, and all who have set an example in my own life.

Thank you to the members of our Military Forces. I salute you. Your tremendous service and sacrifice both at home and abroad, is not lost on this author, nor the continual sacrifices placed upon your spouse and children. Freedom is not free—lest we forget.

Thank you to the following superstars. Without your direct contributions this book would certainly not exist:

Dan & Lacy Estrada
Chris & Rachael Haines
Drew & Lara Killian
Brent & Kimberly McArthur
Dr. C. Brent & Jeniel Metcalf
James & Jewels Montgomery
Don & Barbara Philpitt
Ethan Prete
Ferron Prete
Julianna Recksiek
Joseph Roveri
B. George & Deborah Saloom
Stefani Ward Steelman
Erica Vanderwood
Rob & Lorraine Vanderwood
Dan Walker
The Honorable Clark & Janie Wilkinson

Thank you to the key strategic advisors to *Man, You Rock!*

Bobbie Carlyle—Creator/Sculptor of the world-famous *Self Made Man* statue (front cover image) and Foreword.

1106 Design—Professionals every step of the way.

Blackwatch Press—The highest standards of publication.

Kevin & Karen Wilson—Strategic advisors with possible Jedi powers.

Roger and Chris Prete—Strategic advisors and Audiobook Narration.

Dr. Marcia Vanderwood—Strategic advisor—and the *"absolutely gorgeous woman"* referenced in Principle #10, as well as the woman who continually takes my breath away.

Made in the USA
San Bernardino, CA
29 August 2018